SCHUBERT

For Vera
A sensitive, loving, and caring friend
who also happens to be my aunt!

First edition for the United States, Canada,
and the Philippines published 1994
by Barron's Educational Series, Inc.

Design: David West Children's Book Design

Designed and produced by
Aladdin Books Ltd
28 Percy Street
London W1P 9FF

All inquiries should be addressed to:
Barron's Educational Series, Inc.
250 Wireless Boulevard
Hauppauge, NY 11788

International Standard Book No. 0-8120-1995-4

Library of Congress Catalog Card No. 94-10115

Library of Congress Cataloging-in Publication Data
Rachlin, Ann
Schubert / Ann Rachlin; illustrated by Susan Hellard.–1st ed. for the U.S.,
Canada, and the Philippines.
p. cm. – (Famous children)
ISBN 0-8120-1995-4
1. Schubert, Franz, 1797-1828–Childhood and youth–Juvenile literature.
2. Composers–Austria–Biography–Juvenile literature. [1. Schubert, Franz, 1797-1828–Childhood
and youth. 2. Composers.] I. Hellard, Susan, ill. II. Title. III. Series: Rachlin, Ann.
Famous children.
ML3930.S38R33 1994
780'.92–dc20   94-10115
[B]   CIP   AC   MN
Printed in Belgium

9 8 7 6 5 4 3

Famous Children

SCHUBERT

ANN RACHLIN
ILLUSTRATED BY SUSAN HELLARD

BARRON'S

The Viennese schoolmaster picked up his pen and began to write the letter. At last it was quiet. His pupils had gone home. For a few short hours the Lichtenstal School would be just his family's home again, until tomorrow morning when they would all be back. Mr. Schubert had heard that the headmaster of the Leopoldstadt School had died.

"That would be the school for me!" he sighed.

So here he was applying for the job. He wrote:

"When I came to the Lichtenstal School, it had such a bad name that there were no pupils. I used my own money to furnish the school and pay an assistant. Now I have 174 pupils. Many of them are so poor that I teach them for nothing. Please give me the opportunity to work in a well-equipped school so I can prove how good I am."

But Mr. Schubert was disappointed. The job went to someone else. One year later on January 31, 1797, his wife gave birth to their fourth son. The schoolmaster wondered how he would find the money to look after them all. He looked in the cradle at his baby son.

"We'll give him my name," he said. "He shall be called Franz."

When Franz was three years old, his father and mother moved to a bigger house. Now they had 300 pupils. There was not enough money to pay an assistant, so Ignaz, the eldest son, helped Mr. Schubert. Soon the other sons, Ferdinand and Karl, would be teaching – and Franz, too, when he was old enough.

"Father, there is nothing more I can teach him! He should be learning from a real musician."

Ignaz looked at his father, who frowned.

"I said I didn't mind you teaching Franz the piano, but you know I can't afford to pay for a teacher for him."

"But, Father, he is really good and he sings beautifully, too. Couldn't you talk to Michael Holzer?"

"I'll see what I can do," grumbled his father.

Mr. Holzer put down the wine glass that was always in his hand. He looked at Franz and smiled.

"That was excellent, Franz," he said. "You never cease to amaze me!"

"I must go now, Mr. Holzer. Father is helping me with my Latin tonight. They want a boy soprano at the Konvikt School. I have to sing for the director, Antonio Salieri. I'm not afraid of singing, but the Latin test really scares me!"

"Oh, look at him! He looks like a miller's son!" It was the morning of October 1, 1808, and all the boys were lined up, waiting to sing for the examiners. They stared when Franz Schubert joined the line. Franz felt uncomfortable in his pale blue coat that had faded so much it was almost white. He was small, stumpy and wore steel-rimmed spectacles. He was eleven years old and very shy.

"Next, please!" Franz stood in front of the three judges. Soon Antonio Salieri was asking him to sing and the headmaster was testing his Latin verbs!

"Thank you very much. You may go now!" Franz went back to his father, who was waiting outside.

"It won't be long, Father. The judges are deciding."

The headmaster looked at the anxious young faces. He must not keep them in suspense.

"The two sopranos, Müllner and Schubert, performed excellently. As they also passed all the school tests with high marks, they will join the Court Chapel Choir and attend the Konvikt School next term."

"Well done, Franz!" his father smiled proudly. "You have brought honor to the family."

Before long, Franz was looking smart in his new school uniform.

"Stand still! Your hat's crooked!" Ferdinand laughed as he straightened the special chorister's hat on his brother's head. Soon Franz must leave his family. When it was time to go, he smiled bravely as he waved good-bye.

Franz shivered. It was freezing cold in school, for there was no heat.

"I would give anything for a bowl of hot soup," he murmured, as his tummy rumbled with hunger. "School food is horrible, and the portions are so small!" Alone in the practice room, he took out his music paper and began to compose. Soon he had forgotten how cold and hungry he was. He was happy writing music.

"Tell us how you spend your day!" Franz was home on a rare visit.

"Well, apart from my schoolwork, I am the orchestra assistant. I string the violins, light the candles, and make sure the instruments and scores are in place. I play the violin every day as well as sing in the choir. We give concerts and I play the piano. Sometimes we perform *my* music!"

"Don't neglect your schoolwork!" warned his father. "I think you are spending too much time on music. You have to be a schoolteacher when you grow up, not a musician!"

Back at school, Franz told his friend, Josef von Spaun, "Father isn't too pleased with me. He doesn't approve of my music, but I composed a new minuet without him knowing. Would you like to hear it?"

"It's beautiful, Franz!" said Josef. "Look, here is some more music paper for you."

"You are kind, Josef. Please don't tell Father I am composing. Promise me!"

"Of course. Now listen. Put your music away! Have you heard the news? Napoleon is back with his troops and they're marching into the city. Dr. Lang has forbidden us to take part, but the seniors have decided to take no notice and are forming a Students' Corps to help defend Vienna."

"How dare you disobey me?" Dr. Lang was waiting when the boys returned. "Go to your rooms at once!"

"We're going again tomorrow!" Josef whispered to Franz. When they returned the next day, Dr. Lang locked them in their rooms.

The boys were watching cannon-balls fly across the night sky. Napoleon's soldiers had set fire to many buildings, and the glow of the flames could be seen for miles. Suddenly a cannon-ball landed in one of the fountains in University Square, in front of the school.

Inside the school a deafening noise was heard. Someone screamed! Smoke was pouring down the staircase and Franz looked at Josef in horror.

"The school's on fire!" The boys, pale with fear, ran to see. "We all could have been killed!"

Franz stared at the huge hole. The cannon-ball had gone right through the building before exploding as it hit the ground.

Some time later, the tears streamed down Franz's cheeks. "Oh, Josef, I can't believe it!" The headmaster had just told him of his mother's death. He went home for her funeral.

For eleven months his poor father struggled on alone, but the following April Dr. Lang had good news for Franz. The boy was going home again, but this time for a happy event. On April 13, 1813, his father married Anna Kleyenbock.

When he was fifteen, Franz's voice broke and his days as a choirboy were over.

"Franz Schubert crowed for the last time, July 26, 1812," he wrote. He was so hungry. He wrote home asking Ferdinand to lend him some money for food.

"You know what it is like to long for bread and an apple! School lunch is miserable and I have to wait eight-and-a-half hours for a supper that's even worse!"

Yet Franz dreaded leaving school. He did not want to become a schoolmaster like his father. His kind stepmother understood. Whenever his father gave her some extra money, she saved it in a stocking.

"Anything in the stocking, Mother?" asked Franz when he visited her.

There was always a coin or two for him.

Franz Schubert worked as a schoolmaster for only three years. He hated it! He was happier as a musician, even though he knew he would be poor for the rest of his life. He became a great composer and wrote nine symphonies.

The most famous is No. 8 in B minor, the "Unfinished," which has only two movements and was found in a drawer after he died in 1828.

Among the 600 beautiful songs he wrote were "The Trout"

and "The Wild Rose."